This book is a dedication to

my family

and all

my friends.

Published by Journey Together Publishing
First published in 2025

Written by Ida Marie Artis
Illustrated by Sara Hoagland
Book design by Bryony Simmonds

ISBN: 979-8-9989103-6-4 (paperback)

The Adventures of Luci Light

Written by
Ida Marie Artis

Illustrated by
Sara Hoagland

Today Luci Light woke up
to a fresh croissant and milk.

Outside she sees a magnificent tower.

"It is the Eifel Tower!!"

Where did she wake up?

After breakfast Luci Light
surfs the biggest waves.
She sees Kelly Slater,
the famous surfer, too.
To her delight a Turtle Family swims
really close to Luci's surfboard.

"What a wonderful sight!"

Where in the world is Luci Light?

Later Luci meets her fairy friends at
the 'Cliffs Of Moher'.

Together they head on, to listen to
some music in a cozy pub.

Where did Luci Light go?

Next, Luci hops on a red

double decker bus.

It takes her to the
'Royal Palace'

where she has a nice cup of tea.

Where in the world is her tea time?

Now Lucy Light is hungry.
She visits a delicious bakery
where she tries their famous
pretzels and cake.

Luci learns that this
country once was
divided into East and
West by a huge wall.

Where is Luci Light?

BÄCKEREI

In the afternoon she watches a
big show on the 'Broadway'.

Then Luci takes a train to visit the
'Statue Of Liberty'.

Which big city is Luci Light in?

In the evening Luci Light
goes on a long plain ride to the land
of the cherry-blossom trees.

On her way to the famous
'Tokyo Tower'

Luci tastes the best Sushi
in the entire world.

What is Luci Light's destination?

Right before bedtime
Luci likes to watch the stars.

She sits in the soft, green grass
and gazes at the majestic
'Southern Cross'.
In the distance she hears
the sheep bleat.

"If I watch closely I might see
the famous Kiwi Bird!" she thinks.

Where is Luci Light now?

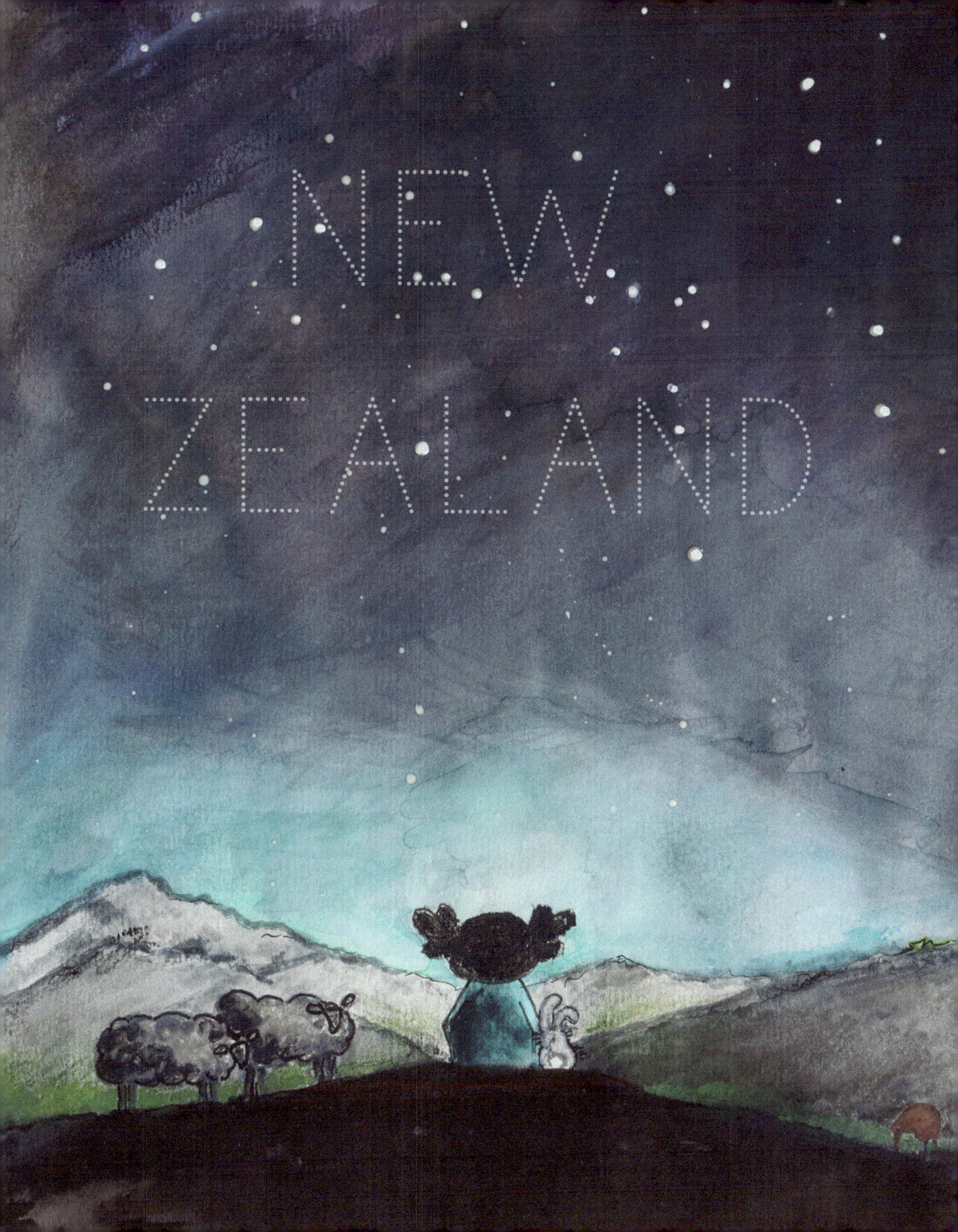
NEW
ZEALAND

Finally Luci is tired.

She snuggles up
underneath her warm blanket
with her favorite stuffed animal,
a little toy bunny.

Where did Luci Light go to sleep?

About the Author

Ida Marie Artis is a young author from Hawaii. At 9 years old she has visited more than 20 countries. Ida's adventures inspired her to write the storyline for 'Luci Light's Adventures'.

While this book is one of many stories she has written, Ida is also a painter, entrepreneur, seamstress and recording artist. Her song "No Weight" featuring Kelly Slater and Jake Shimabukuro was a collaboration with her father.

Currently Ida is full time traveling with her parents and four younger siblings.

About the Illustrator

Sara Hoagland has her roots in Sweden and focuses on Illustration, Design and Woodworking.

She loved having the opportunity to use her hand drawing skills for the illustrations in this book.

Please leave a review

If you enjoyed this book,
please take a moment
to leave a review on Amazon.

It would mean the world
to a self-publishing author
like me.

www.ingramcontent.com/pod-product-compliance
Lightning Source LLC
Chambersburg PA
CBHW041621120626
46551CB00003B/532